I0155449

# Pathways

# Pathways

## Margaret A. Westlie

**Selkirk**
STORIES

Copyright © Margaret A. Westlie 2018
ISBN 978-1-926494-28-9

Selkirk Stories™ and the image of a heart with three stars are trademarks of Selkirk Stories, Cornwall, Prince Edward Island, Canada.

TABLE OF CONTENTS

Seasons of Life                                        7
  Talent                                               8
  Empathic Infant                                      9
  Haircut                                             10
  Whistling                                           11
  When Mother Swallowed the Bagpipe Seasoning         12
  Kaleidoscope                                        14
  Ice Cream                                           15
  Little Girls and Ice Cream                          16
  Milking                                             17
  A Man of Little Fame                                18
  Infant In Absentia                                  19
  My Meggie Anne                                      20
  Life Train                                          21
  Counting in Reverse                                 22
  Monica                                              23
  Proud Death                                         24
  Fit Bit                                             25
  Balance                                             26
  Hearing Aid                                         27
  Old Age                                             28
  Flowers                                             29
  Wind Whispers                                       30
Points of View                                        31
  Silence                                             32
  Earthing                                            33
  Meditation                                          34
  Free Will                                           35
  The State of War                                    36
  Dry Bones                                           37
  Her Face                                            38
  Waiting to Board                                    39
  Geese                                               40

| | |
|---|---|
| Cabot Trail | 41 |
| Hard Landing | 42 |
| Writing Cats | 43 |
| Dinosaurs? | 44 |
| The Post Mortem | 45 |
| Don't Make Me Mad | 46 |
| Brazen | 47 |
| Angry Auras | 48 |
| A Cad is a Cad is a Cad | 49 |
| Someone I Knew | 50 |
| The Obituary | 51 |
| Seasons of the Year | 52 |
| Night Feelings | 53 |
| Evening | 54 |
| Storm | 55 |
| Blue Heron | 56 |
| Biting Beasties | 57 |
| Slatterns | 58 |
| Winter's Dance | 59 |
| Bowing Birches | 60 |
| Waiting for Snow | 61 |
| Ice Fishing | 62 |
| Mist on the River | 63 |
| Spring Snow | 64 |
| Brave Flowers | 65 |
| Writing for your Life | 66 |
| Against the Cold | 68 |
| Genealogy | 69 |
| Pap | 70 |
| Travelling | 71 |
| All "P" but no "Q" | 72 |

# Seasons of Life

## TALENT

They said I hadn't any;
They were wrong.
I am the most surprised,
At fifty I can really sing,
      and play a violin, and draw and paint,
      write stories, poetry and songs.
Novels that can make you weep,
      or maybe laugh out loud.
My characters jump off the page
      to shake a scolding finger
      at those who thought they knew me best
      who didn't know at all.

## EMPATHIC INFANT

Why was I born so small and defenceless?
What had I done in the past?
I was only a child and no one would listen.
I was wrong before I drew breath.
Mother said: "Fight your own battles."
I knew as a toddler she'd hurt.
I had no concept of "mother" back then,
    but I knew I had to obey.
And still she sits on my shoulder,
    telling my worth in my ear.
She says you're fat and you're ugly.
She's dead and I can't answer back.
Her last lucid look was destructive.
"You're worthless and always have been."
By then she could no longer name me,
    but she knew how to drive the look in.
What did I do to deserve this?
It's lost to the darkness of time.
Perhaps in some other lifetime,
    and maybe I don't want to know.

## Haircut

It's gone!
My red hair,
    long to my waist,
    gone in three snips.
They said I was too thin.
"They said it wouldn't hurt."
My curls, so thick and shining,
    lie in a tangled heap,
    to be picked up
    and stored in a shoe box for eternity.
"See, it didn't hurt, did it?"
My sense of self, gone.
My personal power, gone.
Now I must be the big girl.

## WHISTLING

I whistle better than a boy
    against my mother's wishes.
A merry tune plays in my mind
    a melody most precious.
"A whistling woman
    and a crowing hen,
    are neither fit for dog nor men.
"Your lips all puckered look a fright.
Deep furrows will set overnight.
And when you're old
    your lipstick will find every fold
    and emphasize the sight."
Too bad I think, and whistle on.
It takes all types,
*Ça c'est si bon.*
Then learn to play the pipes.

## When Mother Swallowed the Bagpipe Seasoning

She was a woman of great frugality, a miser at heart. "Waste not, want not," was her watchword. Her personality was such that she'd look after she leapt. Too late this time.

As a piper, I had to seal the bag with oils and waxes of various kinds to keep it leak free. I was trying out a new brand one evening when the seasoning hit the fan so to speak. This seasoning was a liquid instead of the traditional ones that were more like butter and had to be melted on the stove. The new seasoning was grey in colour, but after it was used and drained out of the bag it had turned a lovely shade of yellow. I had nothing to drain it into so I used a juice glass. Pouring it down the sink was not an option, as it very likely would clog the drain; putting it into the trash was equally risky as it could leak from the bag and make a mess. Both of these events would earn me a thorough scolding. Mother was also a woman of great wrath. So I left it in the glass on the counter intending to ask her what I should do with it later. But plans went awry and I was called away.

When I returned Dad met me at the door with hushed tones and enormous eyes. "Your mother swallowed the bagpipe seasoning," he said. "She thought it was orange juice."

My eyes got as large as his. "Is she okay?"

"So far, but it didn't have a list of ingredients."

"How'd she do that? We don't even have any orange juice."

"You know your mother," he said. "She saw the glass on the counter and griped that you kids were always pouring juice and never drinking it and then she up with the glass and drank two big swallows of it before she realized it wasn't orange juice. Your sister and I read the bottle but all it had on it was the things it was good for." His lips quirked into a sly grin. "It's good for a lot of things but the last one said it was good for preserving the life of old bags." He shook his head. "She wasn't happy."

## KALEIDOSCOPE

Life's a kaleidoscope
    always changing its view.
One turn of the cap
    sets the colours anew.

Look through this telescope.
See what is there.
But don't glance away,
    at least if you care.

If you care there is hope.
You can own the whole play.
It's yours to direct,
    you have only to say.
Remember the colours,
    the pattern's your own.

One turn of the cap,
    one step in good time.
The colours can change
    in the blink of an eye.

## ICE CREAM

Frozen cream and sugar
    melt sensually sweet and cold.
Sliding over tongue and palate
    they delight the weary soul.
Absorbed in sweet sensation
    all cares retreat for now.
A quiet meditation
    provided by a cow.

## LITTLE GIRLS AND ICE CREAM

What is it about ice cream and little girls? I was having lunch at a restaurant in town the other day and I was observing a little girl sitting with her family waiting for their orders. She was maybe five years old and very well-behaved. One of the other adults ordered ice cream for her. I am not sure that she was aware of the coming treat because she seemed completely absorbed in her colouring. When the waitress came by with two child-sized scoops of vanilla ice cream in a small pedestaled fruit cup and set it in front of her, her eyes lit up and she began to smile. She absolutely sparkled with delight. She began carefully scooping tiny tastes of the still hard confection into her mouth. For a full five minutes her colouring book was forgotten as she concentrated on her sweet treat. It was a delight to watch her.

## MILKING

Firm, warm flank
    curved just so to rest my head.
Heavy shift of body on fragile legs disturb dust and straw.
Cats swarm my legs for drops of milk
    that miss the bucket clasped between my skinny knees.
I know the rhythm now.
Right, left, right, left.
Let teats fill with warm, sweet milk
    then squeeze from top to bottom.
First one hand, then the other,
    until the echoing bucket fills and changes tune.
Hay and straw smell dusty sweet,
    milk rich with cream for butter fills the pail.
A peaceful job to start and end the day.

## A MAN OF LITTLE FAME

Explaining power lines and steam shovels
        while I rode on his shoulders.
Wheelbarrow rides
        and roller rides
        while he prepared the lawn.
Lilacs, grass and rabbit hutches,
        smell of new sawn wood,
        sweet beer toddies after work
        and pungent smell of twist.
Sam McGee and fairy tales
        and Little Golden Books.
Sardine sandwiches with mustard
        on Mother's new baked loaf.
The gritty feel against the teeth of
        brown sugar on buttered bread.
Mother wasn't home that night.
She never knew
        of little tubs of ice cream
        with funny wooden spoons,
        brought home to sleepy children after lodge.
Boiled dinners after church,
        the only meal he made.
A great and gracious man he was
        of very little fame.

## INFANT IN ABSENTIA

You were there so briefly,
    three months at most.
My morsel of humanity
    too tiny to be found.
I searched among the wreckage,
I could not find you there.
The only place I find a trace
    is in my memory.
A blighted ovum so they said.
It made it seem unreal.
A boy, a girl,
what name to give
    a non-existent child?
Where is it now if it's not real?
Is there a special place?
A room set by for tiny souls
    who didn't make the grade.
Have they gone on to other lives,
    to other better homes?
Perhaps that's best, no child for me.
A nursery full of others' babes
    must now suffice.

## My Meggie Anne

She's four today
My Meggie Anne,
A happy little bird.
She flits and darts
    around the house,
Her blonde hair
    flying soft and free.
She wears an apron
    just like Mom,
    and dusts a dust free table.
This tidy room she'll rearrange
    to suit her own design.
She'll do it all again next week,
    and then again next year.
She'll soon enough be grown and gone.
I'll miss my Meggie Anne
And I'll be wearying for her,
This child I never had.

## LIFE TRAIN

Clickety clack,
Clickety clack.
The train goes rushing
    down the track.
It races the wind.
It wins.
It wins.
Clickety clack,
Clickety clack.

Life goes rushing
    down the track.
We race against time.
We never win.
Death lies in wait,
We can't go back.
Clickety clack,
Clickety clack.

## COUNTING IN REVERSE

How far I've come.
The footsteps that I took to get me here.
Does anyone keep track?
I know I don't, though I count 'most everything:
    squares of floor tiles and tiles on ceilings,
    buds on flowers, and backyard squirrels,
    though squirrels won't keep still long enough
    to get an accurate count.
Once when I lay on a gurney drowsy with pre-op,
    I tried counting little holes in ceiling tiles
    until they ran together.
I've even counted screws
    that hold toilet stalls in place.
It gets boring waiting in the semi-darkness.
If I retrace my steps and count each one,
    like film in reverse,
    would I find just the old me,
    or would the me that I've become be there too?

## MONICA

We can only go so far with her.
The road this side,
    a marathon of pain and hope.
She sees eternity now and then,
    her time to go is still ahead,
    we wonder at her strength.
At last beyond our reach,
    her vision opens to a wider view.
She sees the things we cannot see
    and knows it's not so far to there.
She calls to those who wait for her,
    we know she's not alone.
This world she enters is not here
    but never far away.
If we had eyes to see and ears to hear
    she'd wave to us and say:
"It's just another facet of the life
    we live today."

## Proud Death

"Death be not proud, though some have named you,"
    or so the poet* said.
The passing of another soul is but a phase.
A step in life we take alone as we did at our birth.
A passing to and through the veil accompanied by friends.
We wave goodbye,
    they cry, "Hello and welcome once again."
The veil is thin, the doorway narrow,
    beyond, the living cannot go.
But they're not far, just through the gate,
    listen and we'll hear them.
A quiet chat with those who've passed
    might save us many troubles.
Some wise advice from those whose sight
    is wider than our own.
So do not grieve too much, too long,
    we have our work as they had theirs.
A few years hence our turn will come,
    to wave goodbye and say "Hello."

---

\*    John Donne

## FIT BIT

As small as a tab on a tub of butter,
  tyrant of training time.
Built by bullies to track your steps,
  recording success for the day.
I wish I had magic
  to turn those dials
  and save my aching joints.
But algorithms record it all,
  ten thousand steps a day.
No rest for the lazy,
  nor friend nor foe,
We cry for mercy but it doesn't hear.
Like all things digital, it's deaf to our pleas,
  and smiley face grins through it all.

## BALANCE

I sit.
Deflated.
Tired.
My morning at the gym
    exhausts what little strength I have.
A stroke will do that.
It robbed me of strength,
    of stamina.
It left me, at seventy,
    deflated, tired,
    with only determination
    to push through to wholeness again.
Hope is not enough.
I need balance.

## HEARING AID

Crisp crackle of paper napkin,
    a swish of clothing on bare skin.
Every click of tongue in cheek
    unites me with the world again.
The tweet of little birds in flight,
    and caw of raucous crows,
    a whisper in the grass of tiny things
    retreated from my notice long ago.
People babbled in my lack of comprehension,
    not knowing that I could not hear.
Lip reading was my daily occupation
    as I fumbled on in company for years.
Now hearing aids relieve me of the burden.
I hear grass growing as before.
Lip reading is no more a staple
    as I emerge into the noisy world again.

## OLD AGE

Nightcaps and bed socks,
    hearing aids, bibs,
    old age creeps closer each day.
Knees complain daily,
    back grumbles too.
When I walk, the hips work when they work.
I guess it's a trend
I'd prefer not to follow
    but follow I must to the end.
I do what I can
    towards the dreams of my youth.
They still linger on despite years.
A pretty old lady I had in my mind.
I don't think I've made it quite yet.

## FLOWERS

Will they bring flowers to my grave,
    or will I be forgotten when I cease to breathe?
My friend the gardener might, if I go first.
Perhaps I won't go first.
I'll stay behind like some forgotten monument
    to watch the world go by and all my peers pass on.
Forgetting may already be in progress.
I don't remember days or dates or time.
My hearing has already lost precision,
    my thoughts unspoken flee my still sharp mind.
I wonder who'll put flowers on my grave when I am gone?
Or will I be forgotten as if I'd never been?
It won't take long.

## Wind Whispers

The wind whispers round the flue.
It tells me of my neighbour's death,
A man I'd never met.
It whispered when I saw an indiscretion.
She was my friend and now she's gone,
I don't know where.
The man she's with I never saw before.
The infant born without a name.
Disgrace no longer private.
The boy gone bad,
His home was good
But he did wrong
And pays for years, and blames his parents.
All this the wind revealed.
It is not safe to tell your secrets to the wind.

# Points of View

## SILENCE

What use are words when we listen to each other's silence?
We do it well, have done so since the start.
People on the outside looking in would find us strange.
They'd only hear the questions asked
        and answered by a syllable, a smile, a nod.
A glance brings laughter;
Great belly-heaving, gasping bouts of laughter,
That leave us limp as aftermath of sex.
The silences we share speak libraries of words and stories,
Uncomprehended by the world at large.

Published in *Thorny Locust* Fall 1998

## EARTHING

Bare feet on cool ground
    absorb the breath of earth.
It joins with Chi.
Rejuvenates the body with each sigh.
Breath universal,
    never-ending,
    meditative,
    renewing body and spirit.

## Meditation

In the depth of meditation
    profound silence stills my soul.
"Peace that passes understanding"
    opens to a world unknown.
Far beyond my waking powers
    seems another place to be.
Peopled by unwritten sages
    waiting for their turn to speak.
As I listen to their wisdom
    clearer still becomes my task.
I must write it when I waken,
    take their message to the world.

## Free Will

God gave us free will
Not realizing he'd lose control.
It highlights his level and lack of omniscience.
Now creation's free-wheeling it to hell on a bicycle.
God gave us free will,
It was a mistake.
The first of many.
I thought he knew it all.

## The State of War

A blight on our condition,
    a lack of sight.
Most ordinary people don't want war.
It's only bully leaders
    who see slight in every deed,
    one-upmanship makes enemies of us all.
Protect our turf when we should share,
    but sharing goes both ways.
We kill our foe, we kill ourselves,
    our atoms are the same.
Our leaders don't see value
    in lifting others up.
"To war, to war," their cry goes out,
    they train our youth to kill.
We have no choice, no end in sight,
    and yet they lead us on.
To hate a foe, we hate ourselves,
    and so the waste goes on.

## DRY BONES

Centuries deep they lie buried,
    but are they really dead?
In midnight dark
    they may get up and dance.
No longer dry and lifeless,
    they may have sentient life.
Can warmth still be and live
    inside dry bones?
Can we trust the dead and buried
    to stay that way forever?
It may not be safe to walk
    in graveyards after dark.
For all we know the dead could own the night.

## Her Face

It was not a pretty face as faces go.
It wasn't covered in cosmetics to hide its flaws.
It was an important face.
Serious mind expressed in brow and quiet smile,
    belied the sparkle in the eyes.
Quirk of eyebrow spoke of hidden humour.
I wondered at what riches lay beneath the cool demeanour.
One small change of expression
    invites you in or shuts you out.
It was an important face.

## Waiting to Board

The ferry's in.
We wait to board.
Yellow-coated figures scurry,
    talking into radios.
Herds of cars charge off
    as if whipped from behind.
Yellow coat listens.
Radio crackles.
"What ya got?"
Yellow coat replies.
"Fifty cars, two campers,
    and a load of carrots."

## GEESE

Listen!
Harsh honking of geese.
Hordes of them in vee,
    their powerful wings thrum,
    vibrating the air.
They carry them fast and far.
Honking hammers the air
    indoors and out,
    while I am forced to look,
    to see where my fellow travellers are going.
Can I even know?
Can I ever be sure?
The geese seem to know for certain.
Perhaps someone gave them a map.

## CABOT TRAIL

The towering hills
    still dark with summer green
    oppress our way.
A giant's hand has scooped out hills and valleys
    with lakes filled in behind.
Our puny hands now dig and clear
    the ancient rubble,
    allowing passage through to other shores.
Beneath sheer cliffs of rock
    the road lies twisted.
Trees cling with narrow roots
    to barren soil,
    their hold precarious
    in the winter winds.
Like ancient people who must
    stand strong or die,
    it is the fate of people and of trees.

## HARD LANDING

The fly zoomed in as flies will do,
    but landed on its back.
With tiny legs and flapping wings
    it righted itself and stayed.
Wits addled by the autumn cold and landing upside down
    maybe it thought, if flies can think,
    of old age and eternity.
A bit of life force here,
    for reasons yet unknown.
I could have squashed it with my cane
    but its work may need completion.
It's not for me to deem it pest,
    and end its life too early.
I should have squashed it with my cane
    but I must have respect.
A dirty cane tip's not for me,
    not even for a fly.

## WRITING CATS

Can I write a rhyme with a cat in my lap?
It seems as if I must try.
This cat filled my lap the moment I sat,
    and spread herself over the work.
Do I dare push her off until I am done?
I think it's a futile endeavour.
I don't own my lap when the cat wants to nap,
    unless she finds sleep in the sun.

## Dinosaurs?

Birds were once dinosaurs.
It's true so they say,
    they really believe it is so.
If truth does prevail,
    what happened to size?
The only thing left is their claws.
Their strength so refined
    they can grasp and hang on
    and poop on the clothes on the line.

## THE POST MORTEM

Her plump body lies broken on the floor,
    her role in life not evident.
For thirty years she gave her all;
    by cleaning she has earned her keep.
Time wrinkles lie hidden in her rosy face.
So hard to tell what caused her death.
Her joints no longer gave her strength,
      her heart no longer functioned like it should,
      until one day she died with no adieu.
We were left to wonder at her leaving.
Memorials don't fit her,
    a funeral, not at all.
Who would read a eulogy
    to a fat, pink vacuum cleaner?

# DON'T MAKE ME MAD

## BRAZEN

Boldly shameless or impudent,
    also made of brass.
Rudely declaring the right of it,
    to all who don't want to hear.
How do you know you are right
    when you haven't looked up the word?
There are layers and layers of meaning
    to be savoured and pondered for years.
Words have a magical meaning
    that can transport us far out of time.
You can't rise above your cohorts
    if you stand at the back of the line.

ANGRY AURAS

An aura dark with soot.
So many years of hatred stored
	make clumps of black throughout.
Rage and jealousy create red streaks
	that flash and dart and penetrate the air.
The silent screams of rage are almost audible
	to those who sense the signs.
Undirected rage can kill the bearer.
It drains the life from every enterprise.
Success becomes elusive, despite effort.
Failure becomes cancerous to the soul.
Rage blocks life and crumbles friendship.
No one will engage the angry one.
Their lives are empty, they die lonely.
Their legacy is lost with passing years.

## A Cad is a Cad is a Cad

A cad he was when he was born,
    a cad he will remain.
No matter how he picks his words
    he'll always be the same.
His efforts for the trodden down
    will always come to naught.
His motives are not pure and sound,
    his plans with venom fraught.
His aim is to embarrass us
    and hold us up for censure
On topics well decided on
    by ancient heads with tonsure.
I think that he should call it quits
    before his tower crumbles.
Our tonsured heads are capable
    of even better rumbles.
He's not equipped to fight the fight
    with steady pastors able.
He doesn't know how quickly
    they can turn the righteous table.
A cad he was when he was born,
    A cad he will remain.
No matter where he picks his fights
    He'll always be the same.

## SOMEONE I KNEW

Endlessly envious,
    filled with dark animus,
    knowledge vicarious
    from sources ambiguous.
Always contemptuous,
    ever vociferous,
    close to opprobrious,
    tongue is acidulous.
Mentally vacuous,
    or should I say crapulous,
    nasal and querulous,
    comments insidious.
Aims mostly sedulous,
    reality tenuous,
    stories all fatuous,
    sources most dubious,
    no friend of mine.

## THE OBITUARY

You're dead.
I don't believe it.
Not that you're dead,
    that's easy enough.
It's the obituary I'm stuck on.
It says a lot of things
    that just aren't true.
Humble?
Hardly!
Humility hides great pride
    in selves that don't exist.
Intellectual?
I don't think so,
    a wannabe at best.
Your thoughts were only inches deep
    as far as I could see,
    no great insights.
Witty?
More scathing than that.
Gentle humour?
Humph!
You must have written this yourself.
I draw the line at outright lies.

# Seasons of the Year

## NIGHT FEELINGS

On summer nights there is a feeling,
    gentleness in the breeze,
    softness in the air.
Sweet warmth pervades the senses.
Full moon rides the river.
Expectancy lies lightly on our hearts,
    hangs high among bright stars.
Unformed imaginings grow and glow,
    unknown and for now unknowable,
    perhaps never to be known.
Except in dreams.

## Evening

Sunset turns firs golden.
Clouds suffuse the setting sun.
In my sheltered space birds gather
        for a late snack before dark sets in
        and they go home to roost.
Downy woodpeckers
        peck at seed cakes.
Chickadees take their turn.
Sparrows and Juncos clear up fallen seed.
They know with certainty there will be more tomorrow.

## STORM

The sky is troubled.
Black clouds boil and churn
    against the blue.
White gulls float on thermals
    etching their purity
    against the coming storm
    as if to hold it back.
Soon wind hurls itself
    against both clouds and trees.
Great gusts roll over pastures
    flattening grass and flowers,
    forcing cattle to take shelter
    from the driving rain.
The gulls have landed,
    they lie huddled in the fields,
    ready to take flight
    when storm abates.

## BLUE HERON

Beside St. Peter's Bay
A blue heron wades through green algae.
Its narrow legs seem too fragile to carry it,
    and yet they do.
It keeps a wary eye on us as we take pictures,
    a certain distance that we respect.
Our photographic rambles lead us to the water every time.
Blue herons populate each tide.
Are they brothers? Cousins?
We're not unlike them,
    each related to each by some degree,
    and to everything that shares its space with us.

## BITING BEASTIES

If flies would stay in the outdoors
    and forage in paddocks and fields,
If mosquitoes would give up their blood meals
    and eat like a vegan instead,
If we could speak fly or mosquito,
    we might persuade both to obey,
    and behave in a civilized manner,
    long life to all would prevail.

## Slatterns

Maples once clad in elegant green
    have holes in their dresses now.
Their shoulders are bare like slatterns at night
    who wear their fall colours like flags.
Their elegance gone they bravely go on
    until their bright colours are faded.
Soon they are naked and bare to the weather,
    their scrawny black limbs rattle loud in the wind.
Winter attempts to cover their shame,
    once snow comes, to little avail.
Spring seems to take pity and offers them cover
    to hide their black frames once again.
Their new gowns are grand as the old ones had been,
    an elegant green with no trim.
Some thanks are rendered as sweet maple syrup
    and they hold up their heads once again.

## WINTER'S DANCE

In stealth they enter on slippered feet.
They gather and wait until critical mass is reached.
Then, all at once, their cohorts join the charge
    and fill the air with snowflakes.
The winter storm is on.
Picked up by wind, they dip and turn
    on currents from the east
    until we're buried to the eaves,
    captive to the dance of winter.
Snowshoes anyone?

## Bowing Birches

Snow swishes beneath our skis.
Air is crisp with unshed snow,
    the tears of winter.
We slide past forests dark with spruce.
Birds silence as we pass
    and rise again as we slide by.
The flap of ravens' wings loosens snow
    from high branches.
It sifts through naked birches
    that bow low beside our path.

## WAITING FOR SNOW

It's winter.
No snow yet,
    only the threat,
    a flake or two mixed with rain.
There's a sense of waiting.
Is this to be the snow of childhood memory,
    a genteel whiteness
    we can ski over,
    go snow shoeing on
    make snow angels in?
One where we can be children again?
Or will it be one that buries us to the eaves,
    covers the windows,
    darkens the house,
    brings on depression?
Until we bring out sun lamps
    and vitamin D,
    then hunker down until spring.

## Ice Fishing

Where do fish go in winter?
I don't mean those that migrate,
    just those that tough it out with the rest of us.
Do they hibernate like bears?
There must be some about.
Ice fishermen certainly think so,
    else why sit round a hole in the ice
    waiting for the elusive bite?
The fish are slow and probably hungry.
In their chilled minds they take the bait.
It would have been safer
    to go to Florida with their cousins.

## MIST ON THE RIVER

Mist lies heavy on the river.
The farther shore is hidden from my view.
Twelve feet of snow is slowly melting;
    as deep as that and more will have to go
    before we see the ground again in springtime.
The season long awaited will be slow.
The birds outside are ever hopeful.
Blue jays wet with springtime rain fly low.
Trees in bud are eager for the sunshine.
Tomorrow is supposed to bring more snow.
My garden's buried deep beneath a snowdrift;
    a late lie-in for plants, but then who knows?
Perhaps they're ready waiting under snowbanks.
They may not see real sunshine until June.

## Spring Snow

We woke to snow this morning.
Its issue heavy on the ground.
Cold and white it covers greening lawns
     and budding trees and flowers.
It is the end of April.
You storm gods have had your winter,
     now let us have our spring.

## BRAVE FLOWERS

Crocuses are brave little flowers. They are the first out of the ground in the spring and are oftentimes under the snow. As cold as it is here in winter, it is always a delightful surprise to find them poking their leaves a half inch out of the ground testing the temperature. It's as if one tells the others that it is okay to emerge and in turn the crocuses tell the daffodils and soon the whole garden is alive with colour.

Sometimes a late frost nips the leaves and renders them brown and stiff on the tips, but the brave little crocus seems to pause for a moment to reconsider its upward climb, then steels itself for the ensuing effort. We had a late March snowstorm a couple of days ago. Once the snow melted and the warmer temperatures returned, the crocuses seemed to gather their strength and climb to new heights. Some have buds on them and will soon open to their full beauty despite the cold.

# WRITING FOR YOUR LIFE

The following five poems are based on an exercise from
*Writing For Your Life* by Deena Metzger. Make a list, she
said. Just free associate as fast as you can, write the words
without thinking about them. Don't censor them, but make
another list of those words that go together. Work with
them and see what you come up with creatively. I had
thirty-six words when I finished my list and used all but
four in these poems.

## Against the Cold

I reach around you in your red crocheted vest,
    your T-shirt's adrift beneath it.
I will be your hot water bottle
    and keep the cold at bay
    until the morning.
Then we can unwrap and live in sun-warmth again.

## Genealogy

Dwelling beneath white crosses,
    we search for you,
    our soldier boys.
In community records
    you seem like strangers to us,
We are the image holders.
You are our elders now.

## PAP

We search for source,
Our hunger's almost palpable,
    but not for bread.
We wait round tables
    ever reaching for the real.
Priests, our spiritual grocers,
    our religious cooks,
      feed us pap.

## TRAVELLING

Rhythmic beat of wings,
    feathers flutter in cadence,
    to follow ferries.
Searching for lunch,
    gulls dip and soar
    travelling to places
    beyond their ken.
Plain fishing's not for them,
    no matter the destination.

## All "P" but no "Q"

The exercise of folding doors produces pleats.
Provides room for offices,
    or piggeries.
Your preference, of course.
Perhaps with a little levity
    a pastoralist will
        perceive the benefits of sharing.

www.ingramcontent.com/pod-product-compliance
Lightning Source LLC
LaVergne TN
LVHW051816080426
835513LV00017B/1975

* 9 7 8 1 9 2 6 4 9 4 2 8 9 *